CAR WASHING I

MW00805347

A guidebook to motivate you into car washing,
waxing, and other maintenance procedures
necessary in order to keep your car
beautiful

by **Thomas A. DiCandia**

CALIFORNIA BOUND BOOKS
P.O. BOX 613
PORT WASHINGTON, NEW YORK 11050

Library of Congress Cataloging in Publication Data

Author....DiCandia, Thomas A.

Title.........Car Washing for Car Lovers

Includes index

90-81454   629.2   ISBN 0-9626744-0-0

Cover by Andy Sprague

Acknowledgment

I would like to thank my wife, Annie, for her assistance in getting this book together, along with her excellent photography. Special thanks go to Doreen S. Berne and Mark and Barbara Goldstein for their editorial advice. The time and effort spent by the following people is also greatly appreciated: Fred Capobianco, William Cotter, William Eckelkamp of Schubert's Auto Body, Tony Eckmayer of Whitney Auto Refinishers, Vic Kessler of Vic Kessler Pinstriping, Dennis McCullough, Andy Riley of Maaco Auto Paint, and cover illustrator, Andy Sprague.

Foreword

Anyone who is serious about cleaning their automobile should have this book in their library. Well written, informative with lots of tricks to get the job done. Car lovers will be proud of the results.

Vic Kessler

Vic Kessler Pinstriping Ltd. of New York

PREFACE

Recently, while driving down a street in my suburban neighborhood I saw a man washing a car with a 4 by 6 inch sponge. I stopped and found myself explaining to him, one-on-one, what potential harm would come from that method of application. Afterwards I thought to myself, I'll write an article about car washing for one of the national car magazines and even more people will benefit from my advice. As the project got underway, I became aware that there was a great deal more information I could pass on to readers on how keep a car beautiful. So instead of just a magazine article, it turned into this book.

My purpose is to inspire car owners to recognize that as car lovers like myself, they should also know the easiest and best ways to keep their cars beautiful.

Twenty-five years in the car industry has given me that experience and knowledge, and it's all here in this book. Obviously, my own cars have looked their best, using these tried and true methods, and I hope yours will too..

Enjoy reading all about these techniques, and use them often. If you love your car as much as I do, I'm sure you will!

To car lovers everywhere

CONTENTS

INTRODUCTION

Once in awhile, I think back to my past and when I remember my adolescent years, I have fond memories that distinctly relate to my present standards of behavior. Cars played a big role during that time of my life. Recollections of those teenage years bring to mind the usual memories. The relationships with people, the fun and games of getting through school, enjoying rock and roll music, but most of all for me, it was -- cars!

As little bits and pieces of the past come back to me, instead of a kaleidoscope of colors, blonde or cream are the ones that stand out from my adolescent years. Those particular colors bring back special memories of a next door neighbor of mine in Flushing, New York. We had very few things in common with one another, as she was a bit older than I, but she was definitely a factor in my writing this book. Terry Hughes, a stylish, attractive, warm-hearted woman was the first to permit me to vent my excess teenage energy, and she was always appreciative of my efforts and skills.

On Saturday mornings, while other young people were out earning pin money with paper routes, traveling all over strange neighborhoods, I was next door learning some of the valuable lessons I would remember the rest of my life. I mentioned that Terry was attractive, but more than that she had style. She drove a bright cream colored 1949 Ford convertible. Most people on our block had boring family-type cars like my parent's 1948 Chevrolet four-door sedan, but not Terry. She knew what she was doing!

I used to help my father wash our family car, and Terry, liking what she saw, asked me to wash her car. It became not only a lucrative job, but a personally satisfying one. Watching the water bead up on all the shiny parts of her car was the first indication that I was "Doing the right thing" as Spike Lee would say. I'd like to say it was more than just washing Terry's car on Saturday mornings in her driveway, but that's all there was to it. Actually, I didn't even know how to drive at that particular time of my life. She did allow me to maneuver the car out of her garage each time I washed it, and put it back; and let me tell you, this gave me instant prestige in the neighborhood. A very mature act at the time.

As I look back to that warm and innocent period of my life, I sometimes wonder if I should have done more for Terry. Maybe if I had offered to wax her car once in awhile, I'll bet the paint would have held up even better. Unless, of course, someone else was "doing it to it!" I guess I'll never know, but what memories!

Chapter 1

THE BUSINESS OF LOVING CARS

Having started three new auto repair facilities during my business life, and having equipped them with compressors, air lines, tools, and machinery, I look back and realize a simple common denominator to all three. I always built up an area in each of those shops for washing any cars we worked on. An inside drain was important, as was running water, and barriers to keep from messing up the rest of the shop with suds and rinse water.

Since I've painted thousands of cars, and subsequently compounded and waxed almost all of them, I am surely qualified to give others advice on the subject of exterior maintenance. I've also worked as a manufacturer's representative for a large corporation, supplying equipment to auto body-shops, and in that capacity I've seen cars professionally washed, waxed, and detailed in many of those shops. Because of those techniques I've observed over the years, and my love of good looking automobiles, I've always preferred to wash my own cars whenever possible.

For the purpose of certifying myself as a lover of interesting cars, or maybe even a "car nut," I list most of the cars I have owned. Since I've yet to acquire an Italian racing red Ferrari, or a British deep forest green Rolls Royce, my list is somewhat incomplete, but given a little more time, they will surely be on it. My first car was an ordinary 1950 Ford coupe that I did some customizing on, fitting a DeSoto grille in place of the factory Ford grille. All the chrome came off, along with the hood and trunk emblems, and I installed 1949 Plymouth ribbed bumpers, front and rear, and a continental wheel.

Each time I did some modification, I would prime that area of the car. Since I hadn't learned the art of painting a car yet, I ended up driving a dark gray, no-nonsense car which really didn't need much washing. I washed it and kept it clean, anyway, which was always important for my own satisfaction. I never did get to paint that first car before I sold it, but luckily, the buyer and I had the same taste, so it didn't really matter.

Next, I got sporty for the first time and bought my first convertible -- a bronze 1956 Chevrolet Bel Air. From here on the list might get boring, if not for the realization that the cars mentioned are now worth an enormous amount of money in the "specialty" class of antique cars being collected today. A posh 1957 Mercury Turnpike Cruiser convertible was my contribution to Detroit "heavy metal." Then, I was ready to get into my first sports car. I bought a 1958 Porsche, German racing silver Speedster that cost me $1,800.00 in 1960, kept it mint, and sold it for $2,500.00 two years later. At the time, I was quite proud of myself for keeping it in such nice shape.

Recently, I heard they are selling for around $75,000.00. I guess I should have kept it!

In the 1960's, I made a diversionary move towards drag racing` and had a trophy-winning stock '58 Pontiac coupe that was all "business." When things got better in my life financially, I succumbed to my Caddy period. First, a sharp metallic pink 1963 convertible, and then a white1965 convertible, a front wheel drive 1967 Eldorado, and a 1969 Eldorado, before switching to Lincoln -- namely, a 1974 Mark IV. During that same time, as a hobby, I spent some time driving a cantankerous 1964 Jaguar XKE, whenever, of course, it decided to run.

Having enjoyed a Speedster as a young man, as soon as I could afford it, I got back into sports cars -- buying a 1969 Porsche 911. I was off and running again! Then I fell in love with Datsun sports cars, and the integrity of the Japanese cars made at that time. First came a 1971 240Z, and later, after squeezing in two Corvettes, a 1976 and a 1978 Indy Pace Car, I bought a 1980 280ZX. I drove about four muscle cars, two fastback Mustangs, a 1971 and a 1973, a 1969 Camaro, and a very hairy 1970 Dodge Challenger convertible. I thought I had slowed down a bit with a 1973 Mercedes, that I still own, and a 1980 soft top Roadster Buick Riviera, when a wickedly fast, 1987 Pontiac Formula entered my life. It was bright blue metallic, with a factory clearcoat finish, that practically glowed when it was clean. One of my current cars, a 1989 Cougar, also has a factory clearcoat paint job, so

13

that finish is obviously here to stay. As you can probably tell, I loved all of those cars and, of course, I always washed them myself!

Chapter 2
PAINT: "LOOKING GOOD"

Ordinary automobiles are painted so well nowadays, even some of the four-door cars, devoid of smooth lines, rakish tilts, and custom touches, stand out in a crowd with finishes so powerful and dynamic, it almost makes up for their lack of styling. What was once a custom paint job, designed only for show cars, has now been incorporated into the manufacturing process of the most ordinary cars, both foreign and domestic.

Custom Paint Jobs

Before clearcoats, there were approximately four or five color coats sprayed on new cars, and when a customer wanted a custom paint job, the sky was the limit. Spraying twelve to fourteen coats of paint was a common technique in custom shops, and owners were quick to mention those numbers as status symbols when asked about their shiny cars. One major problem existed though, as paint built up, and the sun's heat took its toll, cracking and crazing started to appear.

After learning how to paint cars, I would add a clearcoat on top of any custom paint job for added depth, gloss, and protection. Now, auto manufacturers are spraying it on cars from the factory for the same reasons. With wear and oxidation though, it has to be

15

brought back to its original state just like older finishes without a clearcoat.

Custom Factory Finishes

One must give credit to Volkswagen. They were the first to put such great finishes on a large number of their cars. Their research and development teams led the way with what they dubbed the "basecoat/clearcoat" finish. For awhile, they cornered the market on that bright finish. Since the clearcoat has become a special attraction on new cars and because of its tremendous gloss, many dealers refer to it as the "wet look."

Paint Instead Of Fins

After the success of the clearcoat, Volkswagen introduced another brilliant finish on their Audi line of cars. Pearl mica was added to the painting process and this "pearlescent" finish caught the public's fancy with its translucent-like depth, and metallic sparkle. Because of their lead, we're now into these three-stage finishes direct from the factory.

Nissan's use of pearl as a stylish finish on their new Infiniti line is attracting lots of attention too. One of their new colors, twilight blue includes a mix of pearl mica, metallic particles, and graphite to the basecoat and it's topped off with a glossy urethane clearcoat. Nissan is betting on this deep, rich, but subtle finish for their new luxury line.

Most manufacturers have one or two of these new finishes to offer new car buyers, but right now, the "king of the hill" is the Lexus by Toyota. Their paint jobs look so fantastic, and they offer so many pearl colors, I'm sure all the other car manufacturers will follow suit eventually, and add more colors to their line too. If there was an award for the best factory paint finish, the whole 1990 Toyota line of cars would win hands down.

The finish on cars has truly become as much a styling feature now, as fins used to be on a 1959 Cadillac, way back when.

CUT-A-WAY VIEW
OF A CAR'S FINISH

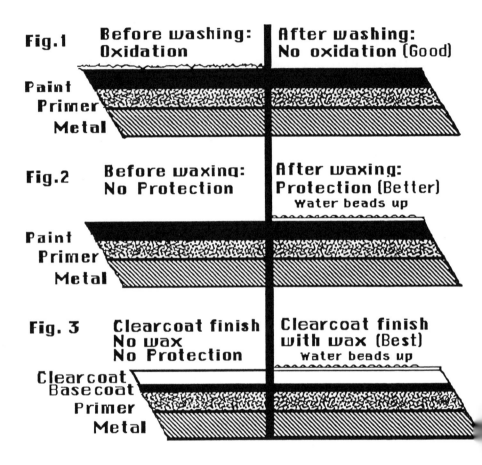

Fig.1 Before washing: Oxidation — After washing: No oxidation (Good)

Paint
Primer
Metal

Fig.2 Before waxing: No Protection — After waxing: Protection (Better) Water beads up

Paint
Primer
Metal

Fig. 3 Clearcoat finish No wax No Protection — Clearcoat finish with wax (Best) Water beads up

Clearcoat
Basecoat
Primer
Metal

Fig.1 Shows standard exterior finish before and after washing.

Fig.2 Shows same finish before and after waxing.

Fig.3 Shows clearcoat finish before and after waxing.

Less Paint Means -- "Watch Out"

Cars are now painted with much less paint, and a clearcoat is applied that gives these new finishes their great depth. With this technique comes some new problems. Since there are less color coats on your new car, and only a thin clearcoat, there is more of a chance to damage this great finish.

Mother Nature is number one on the list when we're talking about harmful oxidation and long term deterioration of a car's finish. Rain, snow, sleet, and the sun too, play an important role in that deterioration. Combine dust and dirt with those elements, and you have the beginnings of paint dullness and the long term effect of a dreary looking car. Also, when an inexperienced person harms a clearcoat finish with a dirt contaminated rag, or burns through the paint, trying to polish a car's finish back to life, a new paint job may become necessary. Keeping your car clean and free from harmful oxidation, and knowing what products to utilize to remedy those problems, takes on new importance as we try to protect these fabulous new finishes. The added benefit is a great looking car!

Although I washed my Jaguar XKE often, this was one day where it would have been very difficult to do so.

Chapter 3

TIME TO GET INVOLVED

Since my last two cars have come with a clearcoat factory finish, I have become even more aware of the importance of proper car washing. In addition to a washing, the car's exterior should get some kind of steady maintenance every few weeks. It should consist of a good wax job, spreading a protective coating to the vinyl or leather areas of the car, and touching up any scratches. All this protective maintenance is an easy "do it yourself" project. Even if you don't wash your car as often as I do, whenever you do, the car's finish will definitely benefit from the attention you give to it.

Saving $ $ $

Once you start washing your own car, you add to the value and the looks of your "pride and joy". Obviously, you'll save money too. You can reduce or actually do away with two to four detail jobs, and twenty or so commercial car washes per year. For discriminating car lovers, who frequent these establishments, that probably adds up to $300.00 to $600.00 per year, plus a possible new paint job after about four years. I understand a good paint job starts at approximately $2,500.00, and even more if it's a clearcoat finish. Since people are now keeping their cars for a longer period of time, due to five-year loans, there's some hefty savings in store when you're motivated properly.

Commercial Car Wash Blues

Today, commercial car washes have become a normal and accepted way to keep one's car clean, and although they do accomplish that, there is a price to pay. Recently I've observed cars coming out of different car washes in the New York metropolitan area, and they seem to be doing a much better job of cleaning cars than ever before. They're especially needed during the cold winter months; but over the long haul, they're not really good for your car's finish.

First of all, the soap a car wash uses is pretty strong in order to clean the real dirty cars -- the ones that haven't been cleaned in months. Car wash operators have to make sure each car comes out clean, no matter what, and that same soap that cleans so well also removes most of the wax from your car. So after a couple of runs to the car wash, you've actually made your car vulnerable to the elements by removing those protective waxes. We know that commercial car washes make the most money when they put a tremendous number of cars through in the shortest time possible; therefore, your car certainly won't get babied and fussed over. My feeling is to use the commercial car washes only when necessary, as it's much better to wash a car by hand.

Auto Detailing Shops

Auto detailers, because of their knowledge, experience, and equipment, do great work in hand cleaning and polishing cars. They have practically become a necessity because "brushless" machines at a car wash, after repeated washings, eventually leave minute swirls, scratches, and a lackluster finish on your car. What becomes necessary for cars brought to a car wash, "once too often," is a compounding and wax job. A good detailing shop can accomplish this, and will bring your car's finish back to almost brand new. Of course, there will be a charge to you of about $150.00 and a thin layer of the car's finish will be compounded off. All this just to get those scratches and swirls out.

During the cold winter months, I would suggest having your car washed by hand in a auto detailing or auto body-shop, if you can afford the extra cost. Also, detail shops have the most efficient and safest machines for cleaning under your hood. Because they hand wash cars, steam clean engines, and clean interiors so well, that's the kind of detailing you should have them do on your car if it's too cold out to do it yourself.

Chapter 4

EQUIPMENT LIST

Start off with a nice sturdy box that you'll fill up with soaps, upholstery cleaners, waxes, and other tools of the trade. It will be partly symbolic, as is a tool box to a mechanic, in getting you started; but later you will find it a convenient way of having everything at your fingertips each time you get the energy to wash your car. It's probably best to keep your box of goodies in your car's trunk. If there are other car owners in your family, and they find it in the garage, everything will be gone in no time, and you'll be out shopping again.

Just like any other maintenance procedure on cars -- "the right tools make for the right job." You'll find all that you need at an auto store, but you can also pick up some items at the supermarket, flea market, and garage sales. Actually a garage sale or flea market is a good place to get started as you can buy your staple items there. A nice thick, fluffy, cotton bath towel that you wouldn't show off in your bathroom, because it's the wrong color, should never be passed up as it will work wonders on your car. Some chemicals like soap, wax, kerosene, and a stronger soap for stubborn dirt are essential, but for those of you who really get into the whole process, some optional materials have also been included.

This box of materials kept in your trunk is essentially all you'll need to wash and wax your car.

Essential Materials

Two to five-gallon plastic pail [the bigger the better] with a handle. *

Large fluffy cotton bath towel cut in half.*

Chamois, real or imitation.*

Large cheesecloth.*

Squeeze bottle of liquid soap such as Ivory Snow, Dove, or a name-brand packaged car wash soap. Actually, one can become a connoisseur of auto car soaps, but mild Ivory Snow is my favorite.

Bottle of Windex, or similar window spray cleaner.

Nylon bristle hand brush.

Spray bottle of Fantastic, 409, or Simple Green.

Gallon of kerosene or a name-brand tar remover.

Inexpensive 1/2" long by 1/4" wide artist's brush.*

Inexpensive 2" or 3" bristle paint brush.*

* These items are easily found at flea markets throughout the country.

Bottle of liquid polish from Classic Wax, Eagle One, Meguiar's, Simoniz, or Turtle Wax.

Can of carnauba wax from Classic Wax, Eagle One, Gliptone, Meguiar's, or Simoniz.

Can of lemon-scented furniture polish.

A selection of materials that are optional, but can add considerable finesse, beyond the washing and waxing process.

Optional Materials

There are many name-brand car wash soaps that work fine, but they are more expensive, and some may even be a bit more powerful than Ivory Snow. If you do use one of the commercial products from an auto store, just remember to use the correct amount, and rinse it off really well.

Wheel and tire cleaner from Eagle One, Meguiar's, Turtle Wax, or Westley's Bleche-white They're more expensive than Fantastic, but worth a try.

Bottle of Lestoil for cloth upholstery.

White/fine rubbing compound.

Orange/rough rubbing compound.

Bottle of Ebony swirl remover.

Bottle of glaze and sealer from Eagle One or Meguiar's.

Bottle of silicone, Teflon or polymer type polish.

Bottle of plastic polish from Eagle One.

Box of corn starch.

Container leather conditioner like Lexol.

Vinyl/tire protectant from Armorall, Eagle One Concours, or Turtle Wax Clear Guard.

Spray can of Gunk engine cleaner.

Old-fashioned cloth baby diapers.

Bottle of clear nail polish.

Sheet of #1200 wet and dry sandpaper

Toothbrush.

Package cotton swabs.

There are a number of inventions and new products out there designed to help you wash your car, and some do look promising. A grouping of hose attachments with the word Turbo in them have recently flooded [sorry about that] the marketplace, and if you've got $25.00 to spend on gimmicks, one of them may appeal to you. Actually, any garden-type nozzle that regulates the hose spray, and allows you to concentrate a burst of water wherever needed, will work just fine. Since it automatically shuts the water down when you aren't using the hose, you'll be conserving rinse water too.

These are the tools of the trade, with some alternatives that also work well. A real chamois is excellent, but five or six times the price of the imitation type, which works perfectly well, and has all the same characteristics as the real one. If an advertised product appeals to you, try it once, and if it works for you, stay with it. If not, you can always go back to the tried and true products I have listed as essentials, and you'll do just fine!

Chapter 5

WASHING YOUR CAR

Whether you've ever washed your own car before, or not, or if you can't even remember when the last time you did, it's now time for you to start. Not only will your car benefit from the pampering it gets, but so will your pocketbook. In fact, driving through our residential areas, and observing many car owners fussing over cars in their driveways, just confirms my opinion that many other people are doing the same thing you could be doing. I've also seen people doing more harm than good by washing their cars the wrong way. That's why it's so important for you to follow the simple rules of proper car washing.

Washing your car yourself is very important in maintaining the brilliant finish manufacturers put on cars today. Leaving dirt, road tars, and chemicals on paint leads to oxidation and rapid deterioration. Besides, there should be a natural pride in having a clean and shiny looking car. Of course, there will also be an end of waiting on car wash lines where someone else does what you can do even better. What better way to let the neighbors know just how much you value your "pride and joy."

All Pleasure, No Pain

Once you get into washing your car yourself, you're going to experience a feeling of personal satisfaction, and the results of that labor will be immeasurable. Aside from protecting the finish of your car, there are also some physical and therapeutic values to consider. It's a sign of the times when certain people would rather brag about how often they frequent some trendy auto detailing shop, while at the same time paying a physical fitness expert to make them work out their bodies on an exercise machine. If you tell those same people, you love your car too much to leave it to anyone else to do; and when you want exercise, you wash and wax your own car, they'll probably want to change the subject.

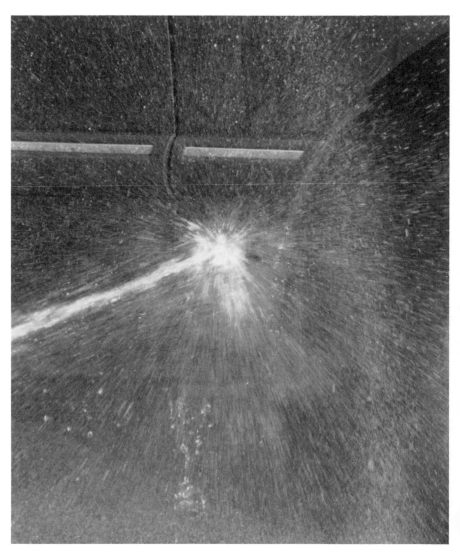

Fig.4 Wet down complete car, but start with a powerful blast of water in back of the wheels. Also, use that same forceful spray on any other dirty areas before starting to wash the car.

Fig. 5 Spray water forcefully into wheel wells to remove dirt and debris.

Fig. 6 An ordinary 2" to 3" paint brush is great with fancy wheels, and it's best to do them in the first part of the washing process.

Fig. 7 That same brush is an excellent tool to get at
hard to reach areas such as this air intake scoop.

Fig.8 Notice the figure 8 style of soap application as shown in figure 8.

Fig.9 A moderate spray rinse, preferably with an adjustable nozzle on the hose, is all that's needed for the wet-down and rinsing of car.

FIG.10 Drying the car with a folded-up imitaion chamois.

The worst thing you could do when washing your car is to do it wrong and harm the car. The destruction of a good finish is cumulative over a period of time, and here's how we'll avoid that pitfall. Buy a fluffy bath towel, cut it in half when you get home, and you've got your soap applicator for the next two years. Use one half, and afterwards let it dry out; then use the other half for the next wash. A wet towel won't release dirt embedded in it from the last washing as easily as a dry one, so by alternating the two halves, one will always be dry. Shake the dry towel out before using it, just to make sure there is no grit in it to do any harm when washing the car.

Get Down To The Wet-Down

A good wet-down is the first step towards washing your car properly. Concentrate the water from the hose especially close to the areas right in back of the wheels, where they kick up sand and grit onto the car. Use that same forceful action on the inside of your wheel wells to dislodge accumulated debris. Also, by hosing down your car first, on hot days you'll be lowering the surface temperature of the hood, roof, and trunk. It would be damaging to the finish to put soap on the car, and have it dry, before you can pick up the hose and rinse it off the car.

Bigger Pails Are Better Pails

I'm sure you can buy a large pail at an auto store, but if not, just visit a local contractor or home improvement shop and see if they'll save an empty joint compound bucket for you; it'll be a great pail to use when washing your car. In any event, try to use a five-gallon pail so your towel can be swished around in a lot of soapy water to loosen and remove sand and grit before reapplying more soap to the car. By removing the majority of that grit first, you reduce the amount of contamination that might damage your car's finish.

A Time To Wash

It's better if you can wash your car in the shade, or early in the morning, as you'll be able to soap down larger areas before you have to rinse the car down. It's best to just do sections of the car on a hot day with the sun beating down on the car. Place about four or five capfuls of soap in the bucket, and then squirt the hose full blast into the bucket till the foam reaches the top. About two gallons of water will suffice for most cars.

Brush some of that car soap on the wheels first, if they're not too dirty. If regular soap isn't effective, spray some Fantastic on each wheel and brush it on well. As you are about to use water for the wet-down part of the wash, you can rinse off the wheels at this time. Kill two birds with one stone.

After saturating your towel in the soapy bucket, bring it to the car's roof and make large swirls with the towel. A figure 8 pattern works well.

Wash it with a healthy amount of suds, but rinse it off immediately. Use a moderately steady spray of water, working the suds down and off the car from the roof down to the bottom rocker panels. Spray some water under the car and in between the wheel wells to dislodge dirt and harmful road chemicals. Then go to the hood, upper sections of the doors, fenders, and the trunk with both operations. Wash and then rinse thoroughly. Next, suds up the lower areas of the car that still remain to be cleaned. These vertical panels will rinse off the easiest. The idea is to reduce the amount of time that soap is left on the hood, roof, and trunk of the car.

Starting At The Top

Obviously, if the weather is cool you can suds up the whole car at one time, but I still prefer washing the car from the roof down especially in hot weather. Now that's contradictory to the way some experts suggest. They say to apply soap around the lower waistband of the car and work upwards. This means that each time you get to the higher sections, the soap being applied runs all over the part you just rinsed. Consequently, double rinsing and double work. Give it a try my way and you'll see it is the better method.

An additional reason for using this method is to avoid contamination of your work towel at the beginning of the wash. Any time sand and grit is splashed on cars, chances are there will be more of those abrasives in the lower areas than anywhere else.

The possibility that there could be sand imbedded in the towel, when swirling it all over the rest of the car, is something you should try to avoid like the plague.

A Time To Dry

Now that you have rinsed off any remaining soap and dirt from your car, spray the towel with clean water and hang it somewhere to dry till the next wash. It's now time to try one of those new man-made imitation chamois I hope you've purchased at a flea market or auto store. They are low-priced, and they are fabulous. Take the chamois and pass it over the car once to get its capillary action going. It will pick up more water once it gets totally wet and is thoroughly wrung dry. Now, wipe the windows with the chamois wrung out, and they will have no bubbles or streaks. Same goes for the hood, roof, and trunk. Wiping down the rest of the car is less critical, but the more times you do it the better it will look.

Soft As A Baby's Diaper

Another fine method of drying the car off is with an old-style cloth baby diaper (not the newer disposable type). Now it may sound odd, but if you find some at a garage sale or flea market, give them a try. Fred Capobianco, car lover and Ferrari owner, dries his car with baby diapers and suggests that they are readily available at Toys-'R-Us stores. They are reasonably priced when sold by the dozen. Although I wouldn't suggest using a diaper for the washing process, because grit has a tendency to stay on its surface, the fine weave and softness of the cloth makes it a natural for drying the car.

Fred Capobianco gently dries the trunk area of his Ferrari with a cloth baby diaper.

I've noticed that many people, including workers at car washes, use a bath towel to dry off a car. It will soak up the rinse water, but it just doesn't absorb water as well as a chamois or a cloth baby diaper. It is, however, very easy to squeeze water out of it as you dry the car. Give each one a try and after awhile, you'll find out which one is your favorite, as these are the best methods of drying a car .

No Place Of Your Own ?

If you cannot set aside a washing area and have no running water, you should be able to find a stall type 'do it yourself" car wash that's popular in most parts of the country. Like commercial car washes, they tend to use a strong soap in the initial soap-down stage of the operation, so use their pressure hose briefly in the soap mode, spend the majority of time in the rinse mode, and you'll have no problem. If they suggest about four quarters for soaping down the car, and four quarters for the rinse, just change the ratio and use as little of their soap as necessary to clean your car.

Recently, I observed a system being hawked at flea markets that's just dandy for those of you without running water. Basically, it is a brush attached to a hose that water flows through. On the other end is a check valve, so the contents of your bucket flows out of the hose and not back into the bucket. It comes with an attachment that clips the hose to any bucket; so all you need is two buckets, one with sudsy water and one with pure clean water for the rinse. The sales pitch is directed at car owners who haven't any place to wash their car with running water. Hopefully, it will be available to those of you who need it.

Chapter 6

GLASS, INTERIORS, AND UPHOLSTERY

Now that you've completed the car's exterior, go inside the car and spray the windows with Windex or a similar glass cleaner. For an especially bright look, use some crumpled up sheets of yesterday's newspaper to dry the windows. The ink used in newsprint gives the windows an extra bit of sparkle, and the newspaper won't leave any annoying lint.

If everything is going well, you are now ready to spruce up the dashboard and any other vinyl or leather inside the car. Also, if you feel like getting into a minor amount of detailing or finishing touches, now you're really in gear. Armorall, or another equally fine protectant, should now be applied and wiped off with a clean small rag. By the way, if you are into household "crossover" chemicals, a spray can of furniture polish like Pledge with lemon scent works really well on vinyl and leather. The lemon scent gives the interior a nice fresh smell also. Keep this rag separate and use it for that purpose only, as most of these solutions streak up windows and chrome.

Of course, you'll empty the ash trays, and if you have an adequate AC vacuum cleaner, one that runs on house current [not some weak unit that runs on

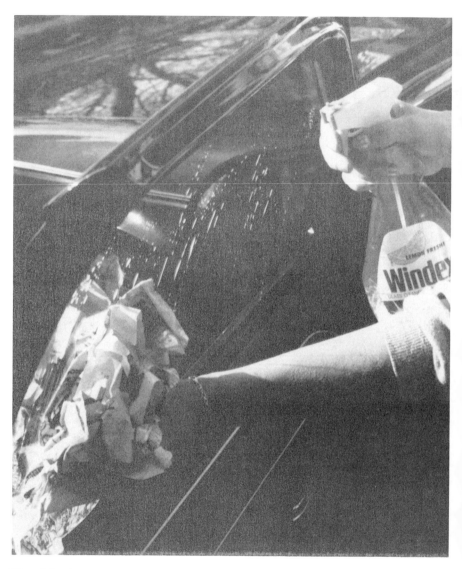

Fig.10 A crumpled up newspaper being used to dry off
Windex sprayed on interior windows.

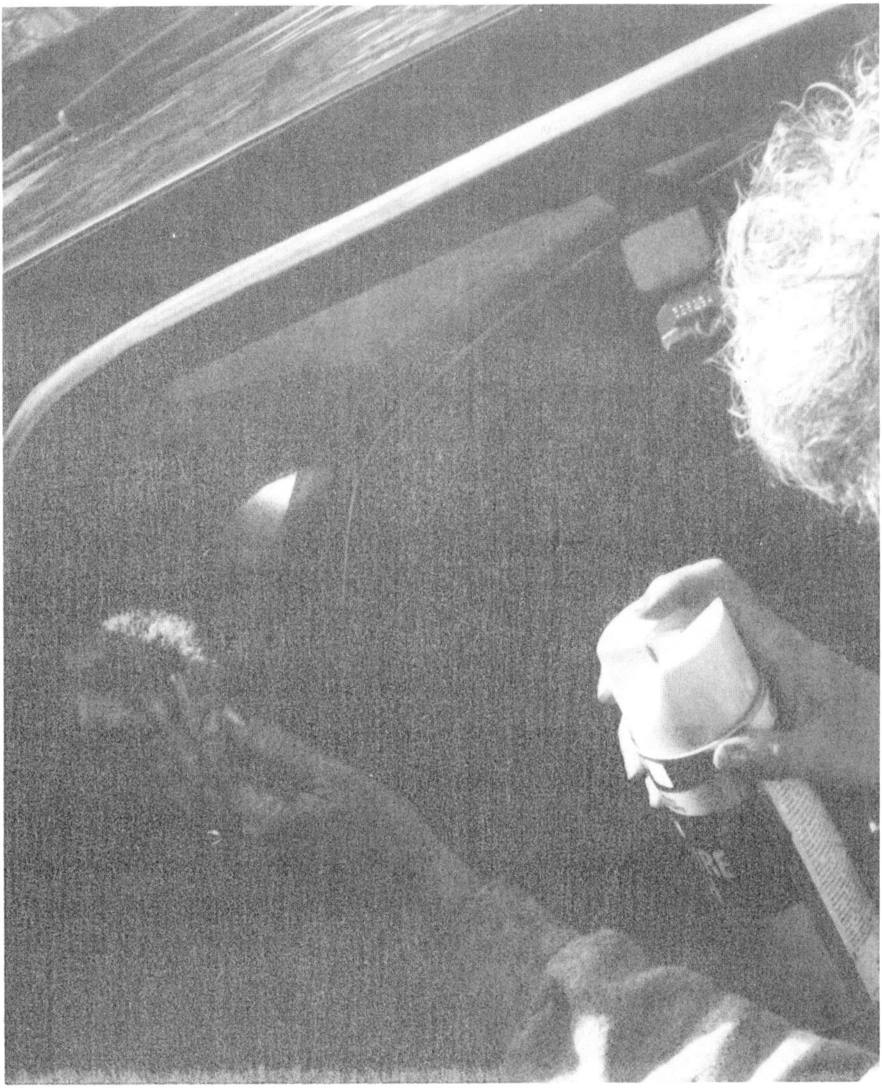

Fig. 11 Applying a coat of lemon scented furniture polish like Pledge spruces up this dashboard, as well as other interior vinyl areas.

batteries] it will clean the floor and any debris inside the car best.

   If there are any spots on cloth upholstery, they should come off easily with any of the household cleaners like Fantastic or car upholstery cleaners made expressly for cloth and velour. Even if the spot is in a small area and comes out easily, you should make a second application over it in a larger circle. That way, you will avoid a ring-like difference in the shade or color where you have just worked. If your car is fitted with a leather interior, you have the easiest material to keep clean. Just make sure to treat it to a conditioner, like Lexol, about twice a year. Spray cleaners like Fantastic or 409 are excellent, but remember to always use the conditioner afterward, as those powerful soaps will dry out leather or vinyl and cause it to crack prematurely.

Chapter 7

WAXING YOUR CAR

You've just finished washing your car, and now you'll want to put on a protective coating of wax. It can be done, but unless it's a really hot day, chances are you'll end up fighting yourself with streaks from water still in mouldings and edges of the car. It's better to walk away from the car after the washing and come back in a few hours, preferably a day later, when the car is completely dry. If it's the only time you have available, then drive around the block first. Most of the water in the mouldings and edges will dry up, and you'll be able to wax the car with less difficulty.

Where To Wax

Always try to wax your car in the shade, whenever possible, as it makes it easier to apply the wax slowly and remove it with less effort. When you do start, you'll have the option of three or four different type waxes, all of which will protect the finish and make your "pride and joy" shine like new. The basic difference is in the length of time that each specific wax finish will last.

Wax Application

Reading the instructions carefully on any wax product is an obvious first step after approaching your clean, dry car. It goes without saying that you shouldn't apply wax on a dirty car. Use an applicator if it comes with the wax, or treat yourself to a nice sheepskin mitten made specifically for that purpose as shown in figure 12. Also, have on hand the cheesecloth for buffing off the wax. These two items work so much better than ordinary rags. Try them, you'll like 'em!

With most wax products the procedures for application will be similar. Use circular motions, continually overlapping the previous application. Apply the wax to a section of the car like the hood, then buff it off. Then apply wax to the two fenders and grille area and buff that off. This way you can stop if you get tired and then go back to waxing your car whenever you desire.

Fig.12 Here is the application of wax using a sheepskin mitten. The overlapping circular motion assures that all areas will get covered with wax.

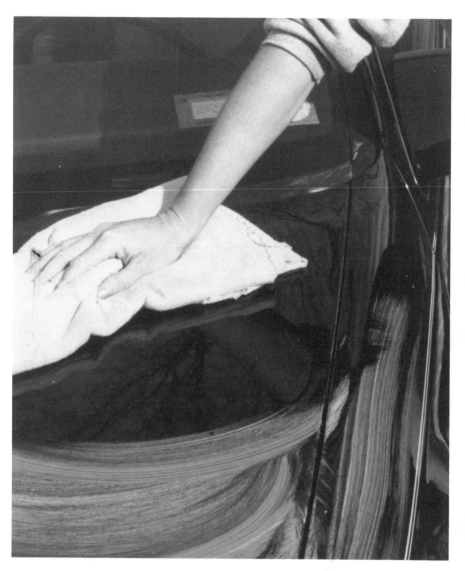

Fig.13 Buffing off wax with a cheesecloth soon after application.

Now For The Fun Part

Figure 13 shows how easy it is! With most car wax products you'll have excellent results whenever you buff it off right after application. No need to leave it on the car very long. Keep changing to a new section on the cheesecloth that hasn't as much wax on it, and shake it away from the car every once in awhile to allow the cloth to do a better job.

Carnauba Wax Is The Best

Let's talk about the best wax job for your car, a bit more tiring than other paste and liquid wax products, but worth the effort--canned carnauba wax in paste form. There are many different ones out there, so the best way to know which one to buy is to read the label on the can. Thanks to "truth in packaging," it's the only way. If it doesn't "flat out" say carnauba, don't be fooled by any claims as to what's in that can. Carnauba is the best, and though it's a little harder to apply, and a little harder to take off, the results will be strikingly better in the long run. You will see the difference in two ways. Obviously, the car will look better, but it will also last for a longer period of time than other waxes.

The amount of times carnauba wax is applied to a car in one year varies among car buffs, but try to do it at least two or three times a year, if possible. Once the first coat is on, you can build it up to a spectacular finish with additional waxings, as long as no harsh soaps or detergents are used between those waxings.

57

One of the best paste waxes on the market, but one that's a little difficult to use, is the old-fashioned Simoniz. Never, ever, apply it in the sun. If you can't find a shady area near your house, drive as many miles as necessary till you find a cool place to work! Under a bridge or overpass is an excellent place where you can work in the shade. Again, apply the wax in a circular motion in a two-foot square section of the car, and remember, the trick is to put the wax can down immediately. Then use the cheesecloth, and buff off the wax right after you put it on. You will not believe how good a shine will result with an old standby as Simoniz, but remember -- buff it off quick!

It must be mentioned that most other canned waxes also have something good going for them in one way or another. Manufacturers keep making these so-called paste waxes better and better all the time. They go on easy and when dry, come off just as easy. They hold up almost as well as a carnauba wax; therefore, they are my second choice.

Liquid waxes in pour-type containers are also interesting in that they are easy to apply, buff off easily, and have another added feature. If you have some foreign spot, such as sap from a tree or bird droppings, that didn't come off in the wash, the liquid waxes, and especially the ones with mild abrasives, get rid of those annoying blemishes very well. Silicone waxes are usually sold in liquid form also, and are packaged in pour-type containers. They're also very easy to use and produce a nice shine with little effort.

Although I really prefer the carnauba-based wax for durability, these different liquid waxes do hold up fairly well. There is one word of caution on liquid silicone waxes. If you have an accident, or need paint work on your car, let your favorite auto body-shop know if you've been using silicone wax. It seems to penetrate the finish more than other waxes and must be removed before any paint work can be done, so let them know about it.

Newest Products On The Marketplace

There are some "high end" items appearing in the auto stores and on television nowadays that appear to have promise as the "waxes of the future." The term "state of the art" is used quite often and maybe even too freely by these manufacturers and their promotion people. Descriptive terms with words like polymers, silicones, Teflons, resins, and carbon based cross-linked formulas are tossed around with such a scientific air about them it seems to suggest that they are the next best thing since sliced bread.

If I were to rate the impact of these new products with the pro's I've polled, and my own experience using most of them, I'd have to say they give a high quality shine and they apply very easily, but they don't seem to hold up as long as carnauba wax. Many of the new products suggest that you can apply them to the car, leave them on for hours and still buff them off very easily, so I suppose that's a plus. These new high-tech products, together with dealer recommended

Polysealants, are supposed to be the future "end-all," but being a "doubting Thomas," I still need more convincing proof.

As you can see from my recommendations, I hate to "wax on" [ooh!] about one particular product, but for now I'll stick with carnauba. Use it in paste form [in the can] as more of gets applied at one time than in liquid form. That way it's the best wax job you can do for your car, no matter what!

Chapter 8

CAR CARE MAINTENANCE SCHEDULE

	Weekly	Monthly	As Needed
Wheels & Tires	●		
Washing The Exterior	●		
Interior, Windows & Vacuum Floors*		●	
Waxing The Exterior	Waxing should be done at least 3 or 4 times a year if possible.		
Interior & Upholstery*		●	●
Finish Restoration			●
Detailing, Touch-up			●
Convertible & Vinyl Tops*		●	●

*At times a more thorough cleaning may be needed

Chapter 9

TRICKS OF THE TRADE

As I said way back when, after observing the many ways to wash, wax, clean interiors, and touch up cars in different auto body-shops, I've learned many alternative techniques which I gladly pass on to you at this time.

A "Quickie"

If your car isn't dirty enough for a good soapy scrubbing, but you still want a shiny, although temporary finish, mix one-half cup of kerosene in two gallons of water, and apply it to your car. Rinse it off just a bit, and wipe dry. Its petroleum base gets rid of most road grime and tar, gives your car a shine, and you end up with a quick car wash with hardly any effort. Because it has an oily base, though, it will attract dust and dirt quicker than a washing done with soap.

You Think That's Fast?

When your car is just a little dusty, try spraying water from your hose with one hand, and pass the wash towel over the car with your other hand at the same time. Sometimes you'll find you don't even need soap when washing the car, especially if you've been waxing the car regularly.

A Show Time Wash

Some show car exhibitors, like master auto pinstriper Vic Kessler, carry a plant spray bottle filled with water, and after arriving at a car show, use it to wash dust and light dirt off their car. He uses the spray bottle as his water supply, and follows it with his washing towel. That's got to be the quickest way of all, as long as your car isn't that dirty.

Double Your Effort -- Double Your Fun

If you have just purchased a used car with an ordinary finish that won't allow water to bead up on it after a washing, try these steps to bring it back to life. First, apply one of the liquid polishes that has an abrasive in it to remove oxidation. Buff it off, and then apply a coating of carnauba wax. It is more work than a normal waxing, but you now have two coats of wax on your car, and it will look spectacular.

Good Habits

A good habit to get into each time you wash your car is to do one extra thing on that particular day, especially with wax. After washing the car, wax the roof, hood, and trunk that day, then with the next wash, wax the sides, grille, and tail-lights. Every other wash, treat all the vinyl inside the car with a furniture polish like Pledge. Then, another time, apply a protectant like Armorall on the rubber bumpers and all the side rails;

also try your hand at some touch-up work, if needed.

If you want to attempt to bring a mistreated car's finish back to life, you have two choices, depending upon your budget and how motivated you are to work up a sweat. Since the average auto body-shop or detailer will only charge around $75 to $100 to compound and wax your car, you might opt for this mundane job to be accomplished by the professionals with machines specifically made for that purpose.

Hand Compounding -- Ugh!

On the other hand, if you are gutsy and want to save some money, you can do it yourself. First, work with a can of white/fine rubbing compound . Fold up a small towel till you have a pad that you can hold onto comfortably. Put a glob of compound on the applicator, and rub down a small two-foot square section of the car. Instead of circular motions, though, work it in back and forth movements until the glob seemingly disappears. Those two-foot square areas will be getting a very concentrated amount of abrasives, so be prudent.

Don't work in too small a square area; and don't think that because you can't see the compound any longer that it's gone. Actually that's when it's most effective, so watch out, as you can go through the paint or clearcoat finish while just trying to take out some scratches. If, on the other hand, the white/fine compound doesn't seem to improve the finish, then try some orange/rough compound and use the same

64

process. After a little rubbing with the rough, go back to the fine compound. Repeat the process and then go to the wax for the final protection.

Machines Work Fast, But Watch Out!

Obviously, there are professional type machines that will speed up the process, but before using one, I strongly advise watching a skilled worker handle one of these buffers. Hopefully, he might even show you how to do it so you don't harm your car when you try it yourself. Even then, I'd suggest practicing on an old clunker first, since some machines produce up to 3000 rpm and are very unforgiving. There are two pads used on these machines. One is a cutting pad needed in the beginning to remove scratches and oxidation. The other is called a polishing pad and is used last with a sealer, liquid polish, or swirl remover like Ebony.

Fig.14 Compounding machines: The professional one on the left, and an orbital type on the right.

Fig.15 Keep the cord draped over your shoulder for safety and the pad on a slight angle. You will not have as much control running it flat against the car, and will take too much of a cut into the paint if you run it at too much of an angle.

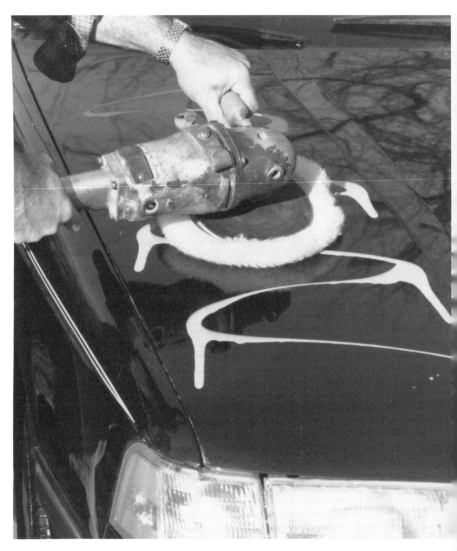

Fig.16 Applying a glaze and sealer with a professional machine. Keep a strong firm grip on the machine especially on vulnerable areas such as the hood, trunk and roof.

You must never stay in one spot for very long as the machine will burn through paint and ruin the finish. Keep the machine moving at all times, and watch out when you get near the antenna, outside mirrors, and windshield wipers, as they may cause you to lose control of the machine. Drape the cord over your shoulder so it doesn't get caught in the machine, causing you to lose control of it. Keep the pad on a slight angle, and you'll control the machine better as you pass it over your car.

Try dabbing some white/fine compound around a section of the dulled-out paint first. If you don't have to use the orange/rough cutting compound, you're better off, as you will burn through the paint even quicker if you're not extremely careful. These kinds of problems are usually not worth the money saved, but if you really want to use a buffer, <u>be extremely careful</u> -- and don't proceed until you know how to handle the machine really well!

Good News -- Bad News

If you're into machines, there is a power buffer that is safer to use. It is called an orbital polisher. Most machines of this type have two handles and turn slower [around 1800 rpm], so they are much easier to use. The bad news is that a wax must be applied to the car soon after compounding, as the finish is very vulnerable to the elements. The good news is that the wax goes on a freshly compounded car with much less effort, and consequently, will buff off easier than any other time.

After using any of the machines mentioned, you should apply a quality product called Ebony to remove the swirls inherent when using those tools. There's hardly anything better for that particular part of the buffing process. There's also a new trend of applying a glaze and sealer just before the carnauba wax job, and the resulting shine is better than without it. Most manufacturers suggest the use of an orbital polisher to buff off these glaze and sealers, so they must feel that the average person won't have much difficulty using them. Just be careful! Next comes the application of the carnauba paste wax and subsequent buffing. With that kind of effort, the results will be spectacular!

Correction Time

There may come a time when you'll leave wax on your car too long before buffing it off. Don't despair, as there is a quick way to correct that problem with another household product you should know about. Keep some corn starch handy with your box of chemicals as it will save the day. It is an excellent buffing aide, especially for the times when you need a little help to get off wax, either left on too long, or wax applied in the sun that won't budge with normal rubbing. Just sprinkle some corn starch on the cheesecloth, start buffing, and watch how good a car product it is!

Interior Soak-Down Time

If, by chance, you purchase a used car with really dirty cloth upholstery it can be cleaned up in several different ways. If you don't mind spending the money to rent an upholstery/rug machine and cleansers, available from most supermarkets, just follow the directions and you'll find they work extremely well on car upholstery too. Another effective method, but much cheaper, is to use kerosene and a good household detergent. Use a soft bristled brush. Mix one part kerosene to four parts of warm water and apply to the dirty area. Immediately after that, do the same with one part household liquid detergent to five parts of warm water. Use Lestoil or a similar type product.

The kerosene mixture will attack oily stains and the detergent will usually clean away any food and liquid stains. Apply these solutions vigorously to the upholstery. If you can get hold of a wet/dry vacuum cleaner, you can avoid the problem of having wet upholstery. If this isn't possible, wipe and blot it as dry as you can with your chamois. Then open the windows just a crack, and be sure you can walk away from the car for a few days. You're really not going to want to drive the car until the seats are dry, but dry they will, and spotless to boot. Spraying some Scotchguard on the upholstery, soon after cleaning, will provide good protection against future dirt problems.

Brushing the aforementioned mixtures onto your floor mats also, and hanging them up on a fence to dry, will work fine to keep them looking new. If you don't track much dirt into your car, clean them about every four car washes. You can use a vacuum cleaner on them the rest of the time.

Fig.17 Road tar kicked up in the area behind the wheels is removed easily with a soft rag and an application of kerosene.

Getting Down And Dirty

Most cars accumulate little dark brown spots on the lower half of the fenders in back of the wheels. It usually is tar kicked up from the road, and kerosene is an excellent tar remover. Rub the spots gently with a rag saturated with kerosene, and let it soak in. When you wipe off the kerosene, they should disappear. If not, some white/fine rubbing compound will do the job.

Scuff marks on outside rubber side mouldings, bumpers, and tires, come off quite easily with an SOS or similar type soap pad. After rinsing the soap off the area worked on, you can make it look like new with a coating of Armorall or similar protectant. The good news is that there's no buffing or rubbing involved. The bad news is it doesn't last much more than a week or two, and then you have to apply it again.

A Clean Engine Is A Happy Engine

You really can't beat a cleaning of the engine compartment by the professionals with steam cleaning equipment. However, if you decide to work on that part of the car yourself, warm up the engine for about two minutes to soften caked-up grease. Engines equipped with turbo-chargers and headers are exempt from this procedure as water sprayed on them after operation might cause them to crack or warp. Dab some kerosene onto the dirty areas under the hood with a regular paint

74

brush. A specific product called Gunk also works very well. Let the solvents go to work dissolving the grease which has built up, and then rinse off with just a little pressure from your hose. It's wise to wear safety goggles, and don't aim the rinse water directly at the distributor or fuel system. Wipe down everything afterwards, and then dab some white grease on the battery terminals, hood latch, and hinges for protection from the elements.

Detailing Brushes

If you want to try your hand at detailing, use a paintbrush when applying the cleaner of your choice. It will do a great job getting into all the openings in the fancy magnesium and spoke wheels seen on so many of the new cars today. I like to keep one in my bucket during the washing process to get at grille openings, scoops, and outside vents.

Cotton swabs are handy in removing wax around emblems, lettering, and mouldings They also work well when sprayed with a protectant to dress up vinyl and rubber mouldings around windows and doors. A toothbrush becomes a neat little tool for cleaning dust out of air vents, controls on dashboards, and other hard-to-get-at areas on your car.

Fig 18 Using a cotton swab to remove wax around this famous insignia.

Disc Brake Woes

Most of today's cars are equipped with disc brakes up front, causing a brownish gray dust to accumulate all over the front wheels. Getting some car wash attendants to spray more of their wheel cleaner on the dirtier front wheels can be fun and games, while at home you can spend all the time you want to make them look beautiful again. Whenever that dust accumulates on your front wheels, spray Fantastic or a similar commercial cleaner on them. Brushing the cleaner all around and in any holes in the wheels, and then rinsing it off with <u>hardly</u> any pressure, works wonders. If too much water pressure is applied, you might kick up some of that cleaner onto your fenders and hood, and that's something you don't ever want on your car's finish, ever!

A word of caution is in order if you decide to use the name brand wheel cleaners. First find out from your dealer whether you have painted, clearcoated, chrome, or machined magnesium wheels. Then read the label to make sure the one you're about to use is designed for your wheels. Some wheel cleaners are so strong they will damage painted and clearcoated wheels if applied to them.

Hidden Headlights

When washing a car that is equipped with disappearing or covered headlights, turn them on towards the end of the washing process. Pass the sudsy towel over the headlights, rinse, and dry. They need cleaning too, or eventually they'll lose their effectiveness at night when you need them most.

Fig 19 Even though the headlights on this Ferrari are
hidden, they need cleaning when washing the rest of
the car .

Chapter 10

VINYL & CONVERTIBLE TOPS

Most vinyl areas of the car are cleaned easily with an application of a strong detergent soap like Fantastic or similar auto related product. There are, however, certain cleaning problems with a convertible top or vinyl roof because of its location. One, it soils easily from tree sap, dirt, and bird droppings landing on it from above and staining it. Two, it is above the painted areas of the car, and those areas are subject to the run-off of the strong detergent needed to clean it. If the roof is really dirty and a regular car washing doesn't clean it well, then these steps ought to be taken. First, wet down the entire car to dilute any soap that lands on it, and then apply the detergent to the roof, working it in vigorously with a stiff hand brush. Leave it on for a few moments, letting it work itself into the stubborn dirt. After you have done the whole roof with this strong soap, rinse thoroughly, using as much water as necessary till the soap is totally rinsed off the car. You may even have to make two applications, especially on a light color roof, rinsing it off vigorously each time till it comes clean.

Powdered household cleansers, like Comet, work very well on a light colored vinyl roof and especially white convertible tops. The bleaching action of these cleansers does a good job in getting the vinyl clean, but the abrasives and bleach can harm the paint, so don't spare the water and rinse often when using these strong soaps. If you can do this particular cleaning process at a self-service car wash, the abrasives, bleach, strong soap, and use of the high pressure spray will usually make any convertible top or vinyl roof look like new.

Last-Ditch Case Scenario

If there are stains that won't come off with soap, there is still a chance to make the roof look like new, but so much care has to be taken with the next chemicals mentioned, that I would suggest bringing your car to a detail, or auto body-shop for their application, rather than doing it yourself. Lacquer thinner and enamel reducer are two very strong chemicals that can clean a vinyl top if handled properly. They can also ruin your paint job if they drip on it. However, if you decide to tackle the job on your own, place a drop-cloth to cover any painted surfaces of the car, and apply these chemicals in an open area, away from any kind of pilot light or flame. They are very flammable, and breathing their fumes can be harmful to your lungs.

A quick pass over the dirty areas with some enamel reducer on a rag should remove the stubborn stains, but if it doesn't, then a pass of the rag with lacquer thinner on it should do it. Just remember how damaging it would be if either of these chemicals drip onto your car during that cleaning process. The drop-cloth will minimize the possibility that any of these chemicals might do any harm. One thing you'll notice immediately is how powerful these chemicals are, and I can't stress this point strongly enough. Use them sparingly, or have a professional do it for you. If your rag is so saturated that it is dripping when you approach the car, you have way too much liquid on the rag.

After application of any of these strong chemicals, and their subsequent rinsings, it's necessary to apply a protectant to the roof like Armorall, Eagle One Concours, or Turtle Wax Clear Guard .

Plastic Is Not Always Fantastic

If you have a convertible with a plastic rear window, windows with tint film, or an after-market sun roof, you must be cautious not to do any damage to them during the cleaning process. They are more vulnerable than glass and scratch easily. Always use the mildest soaps on these areas, and if you want to apply a protective wax, use a non-abrasive type polish, such as Plastic Polish from Eagle One.

Fig. 20 Useful brushes from left to right. They include two all purpose types with nylon bristles, an ordinary 3" paint brush, a 1/2" long by 1/4" wide artist brush, and a professional striping brush.

Chapter 11

TOUCHING UP THOSE SCRATCHES

If you've ever attempted to touch up your car, you are probably aware of most of the difficulties encountered in the process. A bottle or can of the correct matching color is the safest way to touch up your car. If instead, you happen to have bought a spray can of the right color, beware of its tricky behavior on scratches. As many cars as I have painted, nothing has prepared me for the nightmare of aerosol spray cans.

More Harm Than Good

I remember a neighbor, once spraying each scratch on his light green, 1957 Chevrolet Bel Air hardtop convertible with what should have been the correct match, touch-up spray can. When he was finished he had effectively ruined the paint job on his car. His car's factory paint job had more silver metallic showing on the surface than the touch-up spray can he was using. Therefore, every scratch he sprayed became a darker circle of green, each one about two inches in diameter. His car's finish ended up looking like a green leopard. Actually, a little dab of paint applied with a brush was all that was needed. The best way to use an aerosol spray can is to aim the spray into the cap or some other tray, and then use that liquid which you've collected with a small brush.

Brush Techniques

Next it's time for some brush talk. Most of the time an ordinary artist's brush, about one-half inch long and about one-quarter inch thick, will be the easiest way to control the touch-up process. Professional car striping brushes, roughly two inches long, are great for long scratches, but don't work well on small chipped areas. The long brush, loaded with paint, will wiggle too much instead of just being a dabber, and you'll be left with a mess. Always stir the paint well, as that is the only way you'll get an accurate match. Try filling the scratch or nicks with a minimum amount of paint, and as each application dries, apply another one. Applying three or four coats, instead of one, will build up the touched-up area just fine. When you first start filling the brush with paint, squeeze off excess paint into the rim of the can, and then use that paint in the rim, on the car. Its thicker consistency will do a quicker and better job with less of a chance of having the paint run.

A Clear Use For Nail Polish

Car paint has always been a bit difficult to touch up in the past, and now with clearcoat finishes, one more step is necessary for it to look really good. Find out from your dealer or auto body-shop if your car has a clearcoat finish. If so, a small jar of clear nail polish and a small brush will be necessary to complete the touch-up process. After filling the nicks and scratches with a color coat, go over the area you have worked on with a final coat of clear nail polish, and you will have

85

reproduced your car's finish perfectly and protected it as well.

There is a more professional step in the touch-up process, and I'll include it just in case you are an absolute perfectionist . Continue adding more drops of paint until the scratched or nicked area is higher than the finish around it and let it dry for about a week. Then mask off the surrounding area and sand the recently applied paint with ultra fine #1200 wet and dry sandpaper. When you have brought that bubbled-up area of paint down to the level of the car's finish, brush a coat of clear nail polish on it, wait an hour or so, and remove the masking tape. After about a week you can polish and wax that area the same as the rest of the car.

Chapter 12

CAR WASHING FOR BUCKS

I started washing and waxing cars when I was a teenager, and I suggest the same for the teenagers of today. It's a great way to earn money. With some simple household products, as mentioned earlier, and an area to work in, it's possible to make good bucks on Saturday mornings washing cars. Let people know that you are "hand washing" cars, and I bet there's forty to fifty dollars to be made each weekend once the word gets out. Charging the same five to seven dollars as the commercial car washes, and accepting a forty to fifty dollar wax job whenever you feel like it, has to be more lucrative than the old paper route. If a real "car nut" wants you to use packaged automotive soaps and conditioners in the cleaning process, you can charge ten to fifteen dollars for that kind of personalized service, and rather than the regular car wash most people will ask for, you can give their car the deluxe hand-washed special.

Remember too, if you do more than wash the car, clean the tires and wheels, and vacuum the interior, you've got to charge more money. Scrubbing a dirty vinyl roof till it looks good might be a job all by itself. The same goes for dressing tires, rubber mouldings, bumpers, and removing imbedded dirt in the upholstery. I've told you how, and now when you do

perform those extra tasks, make sure you get paid for
them!

Fig. 21 A couple of ways to attract customers to a charity car wash.

Chapter 13

CHARITY CAR WASHING

The obvious door-to-door canvassing by young people, in order to raise money for the annual Muscular Dystrophy and Cerebral Palsy telethons, M.A.D.D., or other worthwhile causes, has always been effective, but not necessarily fun for socially conscious teenagers. It never fails to amaze me, though, to see the fun a group of guys and girls have when they are part of a charity car wash. They start out with the same drawbacks of collecting money, but they don't look like they mind it one bit. Maybe giving the donors such a good deal for their contribution to a particular cause, and maybe because it's a group activity, charity car washes seem to work very well! Usually a set fee is charged, and when someone knowledgeable supervises the car wash, a goodly amount of money can be collected that day.

Easy Does It

For those adults who are asked for advice, and wish to do their part to help, here are some of the essential elements of a charity car wash.

A safe suitable area should be found in order to ensure that no one gets run over, and that regular street traffic isn't disrupted. A hose with a nozzle and running water is necessary and the rest is easy. You'll need two five- gallon pails [one for each side of the line that forms] and two towels cut in half, for the four people designated as washers.

Ivory Snow, Dove, or a name-brand car wash soap, and again, that bottle of Fantastic for the wheels, should be the contribution from the local supermarkets. Four imitation chamois, or two towels cut in half, will be needed for the four people who will be the dryers. These eight teenagers can turn an ordinary Saturday morning into an absolute money making event.

Car "Lovers Lane"

Have some students from an art class make up some posters to drum up business. Place them around town the night before. This will help to insure success. Also, one or two signs at the approach of the car wash area will attract the attention of passing motorists. A sign placed at the beginning will help guide cars into the wash lane.

Finding The Groove

There should be a minimum fee of five dollars per wash, and once everybody gets "into the groove," and they do a really good job, it should bring even more of a contribution from impressed car lovers, if they can afford to give more. When the cars are washed correctly, and when the word gets around, the owners of Corvettes, Porsches, and other fine cars will start showing up to get washed. At that point though, I would confine the washing to just the cars. The car owners should shower at home like everyone else!

These events usually don't have much participation by "macho" young men who aren't ordinarily involved in causes, but when they find out what type of cars are coming around to be washed, this might change their attitude and get them to help too.

In a charity car wash, the contributor gets something of value for his or her money, and the kids, instead of begging for contributions, feel they've performed a community service. Therefore, I think it's better than just ringing doorbells and asking for money. Hats off to them!

Chapter 14

A VIDEOTAPE HISTORY

After speaking with many of my fellow car lovers and owners of video cameras, I have put the two together and come up with an idea whose time has come. There seems to be a desire to have a pictorial record of some of the cars we have owned in the past. I would love to have the cars I've owned over the years on film or videotape. Each car's chronology, change in size, style, color, and the opportunity for us "shy types" to be photographed should make great viewing in our later years. Since photography buffs, who operate cameras, are rarely in the pictures themselves, videotape would enable car lovers to be immortalized while interacting with their special cars.

Lights, Camera, Action

Each time a car is acquired, persuade a family member or friend to videotape you washing or waxing your "pride and joy." The car you videotape today will signify many things in the years to come. It will show your taste in cars, as well as how you look at the time, for better or for worse. You'll want to show how beautifully you keep your car. Action shots of you washing or waxing it will be much more interesting to look at than the typical family video shots, with everyone just standing there doing nothing. If you have a waterproof camera case, it's possible to do some trick photography with all those suds -- just use your imagination!

Check Out Time

I hope I've given you enough reasons to "get busy" with pride, economics, and your own personal satisfaction as the motives for keeping a car beautiful. Also, keep in mind how many other car lovers are checking you out when you are driving your shiny car down the street. If you can do it yourself, more power to you. Happy motoring, and remember -- smile at us as you go by!

Index